p

24ᵗʰ May, 1949.

Gerald Clifford Weales,
Hartley Hall, Columbia,
New York City.

THE SONG OF THE COLD

The Song of the Cold

EDITH SITWELL

THE VANGUARD PRESS, INC.

NEW YORK

Contents

ACKNOWLEDGMENTS

My thanks are due to the editors of *View, New Writing and Daylight, Penguin New Writing, Orion,* and *Poetry London* for permission to reprint certain of these poems first published by them.

My thanks are due, also, to Messrs. Macmillan of New York, for their permission to include 'Most lovely dark'; and to Messrs. Macmillan of London for their permission to include certain poems which appeared in their edition —a different one from this—of 'The Song of the Cold'; and to Messrs. Gerald Duckworth for their permission to include 'Romance,' 'Gold Coast Customs,' and 'Twelve Early Poems."

E. S.

THE SONG OF THE COLD

Three Poems of the Atomic Age

I

Dirge for the New Sunrise

(Fifteen minutes past eight o'clock, on the morning of Monday, the 6th of August, 1945.)

BOUND to my heart as Ixion to the wheel,
Nailed to my heart as the thief upon the cross,
I hang between our Christ and the gap where the world was lost

And watch the phantom Sun in Famine Street—
The ghost of the heart of Man. . . . red Cain,
And the more murderous brain
Of Man, still redder Nero that conceived the death
Of his mother Earth, and tore
Her womb, to know the place where he was conceived.

But no eyes grieved—
For none were left for tears:
They were blinded as the years
Since Christ was born. Mother or Murderer, you have given or
         taken life—
Now all is one!

There was a morning when the holy Light
Was young . . . The beautiful First Creature came
To our water-springs, and thought us without blame.

Our hearts seemed safe in our breasts and sang to the Light—
The marrow in the bone
We dreamed was safe . . . the blood in the veins, the sap in the
        tree
Were springs of Deity.

But I saw the little Ant-men as they ran
Carrying the world's weight of the world's filth
And the filth in the heart of Man—
Compressed till those lusts and greeds had a greater heat than that
        of the Sun.

And the ray from the heat came soundless, shook the sky
As if in search for food, and squeezed the stems
Of all that grows on the earth till they were dry.
—And drank the marrow of the bone:
The eyes that saw, the lips that kissed, are gone,
Or black as thunder lie and grin at the murdered Sun.

The living blind and seeing dead together lie
As if in love. . . . There was no more hating then—
And no more love: Gone is the heart of Man.

II

The Shadow of Cain

TO C. M. BOWRA

UNDER great yellow flags and banners of the ancient Cold
Began the huge migrations
From some primeval disaster in the heart of Man.

There were great oscillations
Of temperature. . . . You knew there had once been warmth;

But the Cold is the highest mathematical Idea . . . the Cold is
       Zero—
The Nothing from which arose
All Being and all variation. . . . It is the sound too high for our
      hearing, the Point that flows

Till it becomes the line of Time . . . an endless positing
Of Nothing, or the Ideal that tries to burgeon
Into Reality through multiplying. . . . Then Time froze

To immobility and changed to Space.
Black flags among the ice, blue rays
And the purple perfumes of the polar Sun
Freezing the bone to sapphire and to zircon—
These were our days.

And now in memory of great oscillations
Of temperature in that epoch of the Cold
We found a continent of turquoise vast as Asia
In the yellowing airs of the Cold: the tooth of a mammoth,
And there, in a gulf, a dark-pine sword

To show there had once been warmth, and the gulf-stream in our
      veins
Where only the chaos of the Antarctic Pole
Or the peace of its atonic coldness reigns.

And sometimes we found the trace
Of a bird's claw in the immensity of the Cold:
The trace of the first letters we could not read:
Some message of Man's need

13

And of the slow subsidence of a Race
And of great heats in which the Pampean mud was formed
In which the Megatherium Mylodon
Lies buried under Mastodon-trumpetings of leprous Suns.

The Earth had cloven in two in that primal disaster.
But when the glacial period began
There was still some method of communication
Between Man and his brother Man—
Although their speech
Was alien, each from each,
As the Bird's from the Tiger's, born from the needs of their oppos-
        ing famines.

Each said 'This is the Race of the Dead . . . their blood is cold . . .
For the heat of those more recent on the Earth
Is higher . . . the blood-beat of the Bird more high
Than that of the ancient race of the primeval Tiger.—'
The Earth had lived without the Bird

In that Spring when there were no flowers like thunders in the air.
But now the Earth lies flat beneath the shade of an iron wing. . . .
And of what does the Pterodactyl sing—
Of what red buds in what tremendous Spring?

The thunders of the Spring began. . . . We came again
After that long migration
To the city built before the Flood by our brother Cain.

And when we reached an open door
The Fate said 'My feet ache.'
The Wanderers said 'Our hearts ache.'

There was great lightning
In flashes coming to us over the floor:

14

The whiteness of the Bread—
The whiteness of the Dead—
The whiteness of the Claw—
All this coming to us in flashes through the open door.

There were great emerald thunders in the air
In the violent Spring, the thunders of the sap and the blood in the
   heart—
The spiritual Light, the physical Revelation.

In the streets of the city of Cain there were great Rainbows
Of emeralds: the young people, crossing and meeting;

And everywhere
The great voice of the Sun in sap and bud
Fed from the heart of Being, the panic Power,
The sacred Fury, shouts of Eternity
To the blind eyes, the heat in the wingèd seed, the fire in the
   blood.

And through the works of Death,
The dust's aridity, is heard the sound
Of mounting saps like monstrous bull-voices of unseen fearful
   mimes:
And the great rolling world-wide thunders of that drumming
   underground

Proclaim our Christ, and roar 'Let there be harvest.
Let there be no more Poor—
For the Son of God is sowed in every furrow.'

We did not heed the Cloud in the Heavens shaped like the hand
Of Man . . . But there came a roar as if the Sun and Earth had
   come together—

The Sun descending and the Earth ascending
To take its place above . . . the Primal Matter
Was broken, the womb from which all life began.
Then to the murdered Sun a totem pole of dust arose in memory
        of Man.

The cataclysm of the Sun down-pouring
Seemed the roar
Of those vermilion Suns, the drops of the blood
That bellowing like Mastodons at war
Rush down the length of the world—away—away—

The violence of torrents, cataracts, maelstroms, rains
That went before the Flood—
These covered the earth from the freshets of our brothers' veins.

And with them, the forked lightnings of the gold
From the split mountains,
Blasting their rivals, the young foolish wheat-ears
Amid those terrible rains.

The gulf that was torn across the world seemed as if the beds of
        all the Oceans
Were emptied. . . . Naked, and gaping at what once had been
        the Sun,
Like the mouth of the universal Famine,
It stretched its jaws from one end of the Earth to the other.

And in that hollow lay the body of our brother
Lazarus, upheaved from the world's tomb.
He lay in that great Death like the gold in the husk
Of the world. . . . And round him, like spent lightnings, lay the
        Ore—
The balm for the world's sore.

And the gold lay in its husk of rough earth like the core
In the furred almond, the chestnut in its prickly
Bark, the walnut in a husk green and bitter.

Then to that hollow sea
The civilisation of the Maimed, and, too, Life's lepers, came
As once to Christ near the Sea of Galilee.

They brought the Aeons of Blindness and the Night
Of the World, crying to him, 'Lazarus, give us sight!
O you whose sores are of gold, who are the new Light
Of the World!'

       They brought to the Tomb
The Condemned of Man, who bear as stigmata from the womb
The depression of the skull as in the lesser
Beasts of Prey, the marks of Ape and Dog,
The canine and lemurine muscle . . . the pitiable, the terrible,
The loveless, whose deformities arose
Before their birth, or from a betrayal by the gold wheat-ear.
'Lazarus, for all love we knew the great Sun's kiss
On the loveless cheek. He came to the dog-fang and the lion-claw
That Famine gave the empty mouth, the workless hands.
He came to the inner leaf of the forsaken heart—
He spoke of our Christ, and of a golden love. . . .
But our Sun is gone . . . Will your gold bring warmth to the
   loveless lips, and harvest to barren lands?'

Then Dives was brought. . . . He lay like a leprous Sun
That is covered with the sores of the world . . . the leprosy
Of gold encrusts the world that was his heart.

Like a great ear of wheat that is swoln with grain
Then ruined by white rain

17

He lay. . . . His hollow face, dust-white, was cowled with a
        hood of gold,
But you saw there was no beat or pulse of blood—
You would not know him now from Lazarus.

He did not look at us.
He said, 'What was spilt still surges like the Flood.
But Gold shall be the Blood
Of the World. .`. . Brute gold condensed to its primal essence
Has the texture, smell, warmth, colour of Blood. We must take

A quintessence of the disease for remedy. Once hold
The primal matter of all Gold—
From which it grows
(That Rose of the World) as the sharp clear tree from the seed of
        the great rose—

Then give of this, condensed to the transparency
Of the beryl, the weight of twenty barley grains:
And the leper's face will be full as the rose's face
After great rains.

It will shape again the Shadow of Man. Or at least will take
From all roots of life the symptoms of the leper—
And make the body sharp as the honeycomb,
The roots of life that are left like the red roots of the rose-
        branches.'

But near him a gold sound—
The voice of an unborn wheat-ear accusing Dives—
Said, 'Soon I shall be more rare, more precious than gold.'

There are no thunders, there are no fires, no suns, no earthquakes
Left in our blood. . . . But yet, like the rolling thunders of all
        the fires in the world, we cry

To Dives: 'You are the Shadow of Cain. . . . Your shade is the
       primal Hunger!'
'I lie under what condemnation?'
'The same as Adam, the same as Cain, the same as Sodom, the same
       as Judas.'

And the fires of your Hell shall not be quenched by the rain
From those torn and parti-coloured garments of Christ, those rags
That once were Men. Each wound, each stripe,
Cries out more loudly than the voice of Cain—
Saying, 'Am I my brother's keeper?' Think! When the last clamour
       of the Bought and Sold,
The agony of Gold
Is hushed. . . . When the last Judas-kiss
Has died upon the cheek of the Starved Man Christ, those ashes
       that were Men
Will rise again
To be our Fires upon the Judgment Day.
And yet—who dreamed that Christ has died in vain?
He walks again on the Seas of Blood, He comes in the terrible
       Rain.

                         May, 1946

III

The Canticle of the Rose

THE Rose upon the wall
Cries—'I am the voice of Fire:
And in me grows
The pomegranate splendour of Death, the ruby garnet almandine
Dews: Christ's wounds in me shine!

I rise upon my stem,
The Flower, the whole Plant-being, produced by Light,
With all Plant-systems and formations . . . as in Fire
All elements dissolve, so in one bright
Ineffable essence all Plant-being dissolves to make the Flower.

My stem rises bright:
Organic water polarized to the dark
Earth-centre, and to Light.'

Below that wall, in Famine Street,
There is nothing left but the heart to eat

And the Shade of Man. . . . Buyers and sellers cry:
'Speak not the name of Light. . . .
Her name is Madness now . . . Though we are black beneath
          her kiss
As if she were the Sun, we name her, Night . . .
She has condemned us, and decreed that Man must die.'

There was a woman combing her long hair
To the rhythm of the river flowing. . . .
She sang, 'All things will end—
Like the sound of Time in my veins growing,
The hump on the dwarf, the mountain on the plain,
The fixed red of the rose and the rainbow's red,
The fires of the heart, the wandering planet's pain,
All loss, all gain—
Yet will the world remain.'

The song died in the Ray. . . . Where is she now?
Dissolved and gone—
And only her red shadow stains the unremembering stone.

And in Famine Street the sellers cry
'What will you buy?

A dress for the Bride?'
(But all the moulds of Generation died
Beneath that Ray).

                        'Or a winding-sheet?'
(Outworn . . . the Dead have nothing left to hide.)

'Then buy,' said the Fate arisen from Hell—
(That thing of shreds and patches)
'A box of matches.
For the machine that generated warmth
Beneath your breast is dead. . . . You need a fire
To warm what lies upon your bone . . .
Not all the ashes of your brother Men
Will kindle that again—
Nor all the world's incendiaries!
Who buys—who buys?
Come, give me pence to lay upon my staring lidless eyes!'

But high upon the wall
The Rose where the Wounds of Christ are red
Cries to the Light—
'See how I rise upon my stem, ineffable bright
Effluence of bright essence. . . . From my little span
I cry of Christ, Who is the ultimate Fire
Who will burn away the cold in the heart of Man.
Springs come, springs go. . . .
"I was reddere on Rode than the Rose in the rayne". . .
"This smell is Crist, clepid the plantynge of the Rose in Jericho."'

21

A Song at Morning

THE weeping rose in her dark night of leaves
Sighed 'Dark is my heart, and dark my secret love—
Show not the fire within your heart its light—
For to behold a rainbow in the night
Shall be the presage of your overthrow.'

But morning came, and the great dews; then her philosophies
Of the heart's darkness died. And from the chrysalis of my thin
        sleep
That lay like light or dew upon my form
I rose and wrapped my wings about me, went
From the porphyrian darkness. Like the rose

I too was careless in the morning dews,
Seeing the dead and the dead hour return
To forgive the stain on our hands. I too at morning
Am like the rose who shouts of the red joys and redder sorrows
Fallen from young veins and heartsprings that once held
The world's incendiarism and the redness of summer,
The hope of the rose. For soon will come the morrow
When ancient Prudence and her wintery dream
Will be no more than the rose's idleness. . . .
The light of tears shall only seem the rose's light
—Nor sorrow darker than her night of leaves.

The Two Loves

TO PAVEL TCHELITCHEW AND HIS WORK IN PROGRESS

I

THE dead woman black as thunder, upright in the Spring's great
    shroud
Of flowers and lightnings, snows and sins and sorrows, cried like
    the loud
Noise of Spring that breaks in heart and bud . . .
'Oh, should you pass—
Come not to this ground with your living lass:
For I have a light to see you by!
Is it the Burning Bush?
Is it Damnation's Fire? . . .
Or the old aching heart with its desire?
I only know I tried to bless
But felt that terrible fire burn to the bone—
Beneath Time's filthy dress.'

II

But where are the seeds of the Universal Fire
To burn the roots of Death in the world's cold heart?
The earth of my heart was broken and gaped low
As the fires beneath the equator of my veins.
And I thought the seeds of Fire should be let loose
Like the solar rains—
The light that lies deep in the heart of the rose;
And that the bloom from the fallen spring of the world

23

Would come again to the cheek grown famine-white
As winter frost—
Would come again to the heart whose courage is lost
From hunger. When in this world
Will the cold heart take fire? In the hour when the sapphire of
           the bone—
That hard and precious fire wrung from the earth—
And the sapphire tears the heavens weep shall be made one.

But in the summer great should be the sun of the heart
And great is the heat of the fires from elementary and terrestrial
           nature—
Ripening the kernel of amethysts in the sun of the peach—
The dancing seas in the heart of the apricot.
The earth, the sun, the heart, have so many fires,
It is a great wonder
That the whole world is not consumed. In such a heat of the earth,
           under
The red bough, the Colossus of rubies the first husbandman and
           grave-digger, the red Adam,
Dug from the earth of his own nature, the corn effigy
Of a long-buried country god, encrusted with earth-virtues,
And brought to a new birth
The ancient wisdom hiding behind heat and laughter,
Deep-rooted in Death's earth.

Gone is that heat. But this is the hour of brotherhood, the warmth
           that comes
To the rejected by Life—the shadow with no eyes—
Young Icarus with the broken alar bones
And the sapped and ageing Atlas of the slums
Devoured by the days until all days are done—
To the Croesus of the breadline, gold from the sun,
And the lover seeing in Woman the rankness of Nature—

A monstrous Life-force, the need of procreation
Devouring all other life . . . or Gravity's force
Drawing him down to the centre of his earth.
These sprawl together in the sunlight—the negation
Of Life, fag-ends of Ambition, wrecks of the heart,
Lumps of the world, and bones left by the Lion.
Amid the assembly of young laughing roses
They wait for a re-birth
Under the democratic sun, enriching all, rejecting no one. . . .
But the smile of youth, the red mouth of the flower
Seem the open wounds of a hunger that is voiceless—
And on their lips lies the dust of Babel's city;
And the sound of the heart is changed to the noise of revolutions—
The hammer of Chaos destroying and rebuilding
Small wingless hopes and fears in the light of the Sun.
Who dreamed when Nature should be heightened to a fever—
The ebullition of her juices and humours—
The war of creed and creed, of starved and starver—
The light would return to the cheek, and a new Word
Would take the place of the heart?
                              We might tell the blind
The hue of the flower, or the philosopher
What distance is, in the essence of its being—
But not the distance between the hearts of Men.

I see Christ's wounds weep in the Rose on the wall.
Then I who nursed in my earth the dark red seeds of Fire—
The pomegranate grandeur, the dark seeds of Death—
Felt them change to the light and fire in the heart of the rose. . . .
And I thought of the umbilical cords that bind us to strange suns
And causes . . . of Smart the madman who was born
To bless Christ with the Rose and his people, a nation
Of living sweetness . . . of Harvey who blessed Christ with the
          solar fire in the veins,

25

And Linnaeus praising Him with the wingèd seed!—
Men born for the Sun's need—
Yet theirs are the hymns to God who walks in darkness.
And thinking of the age-long sleep, then brought to the light's
      birth
Of terrestrial nature generated far
From heaven . . . the argillaceous clays, the zircon and sapphire
Bright as the tears of heaven, but deep in earth—
And of the child of the four elements,
The plant—organic water polarised to the earth's centre—
And to the light:—the stem and root, the water-plant and earth-
      plant;
The leaf, the child of air; the flower, the plant of fire—
And of One who contracted His Immensity
And shut Himself in the scope of a small flower
Whose root is clasped in darkness . . . God in the span
Of the root and light-seeking corolla . . . with the voice of Fire
      I cry—
Will He disdain that flower of the world, the heart of Man?

A Hymn to Venus

An old woman speaks:

'Lady, beside the great green wall of Sea
I kneel to make my plea

To you, great Rose of the world. . . . Beyond the seeds of petri-
        faction, Gorgon of itself,
Behind the face bright as the Rose—I pray
To the seeds of fire in the veins that should
Hold diamonds, iris, beryls, for their blood;

Since you are grown old too, and should be cold—
Although the heat of the air
Has the motion of fire
And light bears in its heart
A cloud of colour. . . . Where

The great heat ripens in the mine
Of the body's earth, ruby, garnet, and almandine,
And in the dark cloud of the blood still grows
The rainbow, with the ruby and the rose.

Pity me then—a poor old woman who must wear a rag
Of Time's filth for a dress. . . .
Oh, who would care to hold
That miserly rag now!

So I, whose nights were violent as the buds
And roots of Spring, was taken by the cold,

Have only the cold for lover. Speak then to my dust!
Tell me that nothing dies
But only suffers change—
And Folly may grow wise.

So we shall be transmuted—you who have grown chill, and I
Unto whose heart
My love preferred a heart like a winding-sheet of clay
—Fearing my fires would burn his body away.

Gone are your temples that were bright with heat:
But still I kneel at the feet
Of you who were built through aeons by a million lives,
Whispers and instincts, under the coralline light
That seems the great zone of sea-depths.

                              Though your grief
In my blood grows
Like chlorophyll in the veins of the deep rose,

Our beauty's earthly dress
(Shrunk now to dust) shall move through all degrees
Of life, from mineral to plant, and from still rock to the green
            laughing seas,

From life's first trance, the mineral consciousness
That is deep blankness inside an invisible
And rigid box—defined, divisible,

And separate from its sheath—(breathe not too deep
If you would know the mineral's trancèd sleep . . .
So measure Time that you, too, are apart
And are not conscious of the living heart)—

To the plant that seeks the light that is its lover
And knows not separation between cover
And sentience . . . the Sun's heat and the dew's chill
It knows in sleep with an undreaming thrill;

And colour breathes that is reflected light.
The ray and perfume of the Sun are white:
But when these intermingle as in love
With earth-bound things, the dream begins to move;

And colour that sleeps as in a dreamless cloud
Deep in the mineral trance within that shroud
Then to a fluid changes, grows
Deep in the stem and leaves of the dark rose.

So could the ruby almandine and garnet move
From their great trance into a dreaming sleep,
They might become the rose whose perfume deep
Grows in Eternity, yet is
Still unawakened for its ephemeral love
Beneath the great light's kiss.

The rose might seek the untamed rainbow through
The remembering Eden of a drop of dew—
Until at last in heavenly friendship grows
The ruby and the rainbow and the rose.

Nor will the one more precious than the other be,
Or make more rich the Shadow's treasury.

So, Lady, you and I
And the other wrecks of the heart, left by the fangs of the Lion,
Shall know all transmutations, each degree.

29

Our apish skeletons, clothed with rubies by the light,
Are not less bright
In the Sun's eye than is the Rose . . . and youth, and we,
Are but waves of Time's sea:

Folly and wisdom have dust equal-sweet,
And in the porphyry shade
Of this world's noon
The Poor seem Dives burning in his robes bright as the Rose—
Such transmutations even the brief moment made.'

Dido's Song

TO MARGARET DREW

My Sun of Death is to the deep, reversedly,
What the great Sun of heaven is to the height,
In the violent heat
When Sirius comes to lie at the Sun's feet.
My Sun of Death is all depth, heaven's Sun
All height, and the air of the whole world lies between
Those Suns.—
        Now only the Dog sits by my bier
Where I lie flaming from my heart. The five dogs of the senses
Are no more hunting now.
For after the conflagration of the summer
Of youth, and its violent Suns,
My veins of life that seemed so high, the pouring rivers
Of Africa and Asia were but brooks to them,
Were quenched, and Time like fire
Had changed the bone to knotted rubies like the horizons of the
        light;
Beyond all summers lies the peony bud
Of the veins, and the great paeons of the blood,
The empery of the rose.
Yet once I had thought my bed of love my bier the highest
Sun of heaven, the height where Sirius is flaming,
And then I thought it Death's Sun, and that there was no deep
Below. . . . But now I know
That even the hunters in the heart and in the heaven
At last must sleep.

Mary Stuart to James Bothwell

CASKET LETTER NO. 2

'O you who are my heavenly pain of hell,
My element, my Paradise of the First Man
That knows not sin—the eternity wherein I dwell!
Before the Flood were you not my primeval clay?
Did you not shape me from that chaos to the form
Of that which *men* call Murder—*I*, the light of the First Day?

Leaving you, I was sundered like the sea.
Departed from the place where I left my heart,
I was as small as any body may be
Whose heart is gone—small as the shade of Spring
That has no heart.

                My mate, the leper-King,
White as a man of diamonds, spotted over
With the ermines of God's wrath for a kingly robe—
My leper-stick of bone
Covered with melting snows, to which I am crucified,
Saw not Death gape wide
Wearing my smile, and bade me come again as his lover.

I was the thunder of the seas within man's blood, and the world's
           wonder.
But he sold my kiss for that of the fair-skinned Sickness
Who melted him away like the spring snows:
The bite of the bright-spotted leopard from Hell's thickets, this
           he chose!

She devoured his bones like fire . . . the bite that tore him
        asunder
Hidden behind the mouth of the ultimate rose.

I lodged him in a beggar's house, Death-low,
And ragged as a leper's flesh. . . . Then, weeping like the Spring
From amid his melting snow,
He begged me watch by him, night-long. Did I not know
His heart is wax
While mine is diamond that no blow can break
—But only the touch of your hand. . . . I had pitied those lidless
        eyes that must wake
Until Death seal them, mimicking my kiss.

But how should Pity stand between you and me!
The Devil sunder us from our mates, and God
Knit us together
Until nor man nor devil could tell lover from lover
In our heaven of damnation! Could these sunder our clay,
Or the seas of our blood? As well might they part the fires
That would burn to the bottom of Hell. . . . But there *is* no
        Hell—
We have kissed it away!

Two Variations on a Theme

I

Most Lovely Shade

Most lovely Dark, my Aethiopia born
Of the shade's richest splendour, leave not me
Where in the pomp and splendour of the shade
The dark air's leafy plumes no more a lulling music made.

Dark is your fleece, and dark the airs that grew
Amid those weeping leaves.
Plantations of the East drop precious dew
That, ripened by the light, rich leaves perspire.
Such are the drops that from the dark airs' feathers flew.

Most lovely Shade . . . Syrinx and Dryope
And that smooth nymph that changed into a tree
Are dead . . . the shade, that Aethiopia, sees
Their beauty make more bright its treasuries—
Their amber blood in porphyry veins still grows
Deep in the dark secret of the rose
And in the smooth stem of many a weeping tree,
And in your beauty grows.

Come, then, my pomp and splendour of the shade,
Most lovely cloud that the hot sun made black
As dark-leaved airs—
                    Come, then, O precious cloud,
Lean to my heart: no shade of a rich tree
Shall pour such splendour as your heart to me.

II

Romance

FOR RÉE GORER

SHE grew within his heart as the flushed rose
In the green heat of the long summer grows
Deep in the sorrowful heaven of her leaves.
And this song only is the sound that grieves
When the gold-fingered wind from the green veins
Of the rich rose deflowers her amber blood,
The sharp green rains.
Such is the song, grown from a sleepy head,
Of lovers in a country paradise—
You shall not find it where a song-bird flies,
Nor in the sound that in a bird-throat grieves;
—Its chart lies not in maps on strawberry leaves.

Green were the pomp and pleasure of the shade
Wherein they dwelt; like country temples green
The huge leaves bear a dark-mosaic'd sheen
Like gold on forest temples richly laid.

In that smooth darkness, the gourds dark as caves
Hold thick gold honey for their fountain waves,

Figs, dark and wrinkled as Silenus, hold
Rubies and garnets, and the melons, cold

Waves dancing. . . .
            When the day first gleaned the sun's corn-sheaves
They walked among those temples of the leaves

And the rich heat had made them black as cloud
Or smooth-leaved trees; they lay by waters loud,
And gold-stringed cithern of loud waters made
A madrigal, a country serenade.

But Time drifts by as the long-plumaged winds
And the dark swans whose plumes seem weeping leaves
In the shade's richest splendour—these drift by.
And sometimes he would turn to her and sigh:

'The bright swans leave the wave . . . so leave not me,
With Aethiopia, smooth Aërope:
Amid the pomp and splendour of the shade
Their rich and leafy plumes a lulling music made.

Dark are their plumes, and dark the airs that grew
Amid those weeping leaves.
Plantations of the East drop precious dew
That, ripened by the light, rich leaves perspire,
Such are the drops that from the bright swans' feathers flew.

Come, then, my pomp and pleasure of the shade,
Most lovely cloud that the hot sun made black
As dark-leaved swans.
                    Come, then, O precious cloud,
Lean to my heart. No shade of some rich tree
Shall pour such splendour as your heart to me.'

So these two lovers dreamed the time away
Beside smooth waters like the honey waves
In the ripe melons that are dark as caves;
Eternity seemed but a summer day.

And they forgot, seeing the Asian train
Of waves upon the glittering wide sea main
And rich gold waves from fountain caverns run,
That all the splendour of the eastern sun,

And many a rose-shaped heart, must lie beneath
The maps on strawberry leaves dark green as snows,
With amber dust that was a nymph or rose—

And worlds more vast lie ruined by sad Time
That is the conqueror of our green clime.

For even the beasts eschew the shrunken heart
That dieth of itself, small deaths devour—
(Or that worm mightier than death's—the small corroding hour.)

How ancient is the Worm, companionless
As the black dust of Venus? Dulled to this
And loathèd as the Worm, she is alone
Though all the morbid suns lay in her kiss.

How old, the small undying snake that wreathes
Round lips and eyes, now that the kiss has gone?
In that last night, when we, too, are alone,
We have, for love that seemed eternity,
The old unchanging memory of the bone—
That porphyry whence grew the summer rose.

Most ancient is the Worm—more old than Night
Or the first music heard among the trees
And the unknown horizons' harmonies
Where the huge suns come freshened. Shrunk and cold
Is he, like Venus blackened, noseless, old.

Yet all immensities lie in his strong
Embrace, horizons that no sight hath known,
The veins whose sea had heard the siren song
And worlds that grew from an immortal kiss.

And still their love amid this green world grieves:
'The gold light drips like myrrh upon the leaves
And fills with gold those chambers of the South
That were your eyes, that honeycomb, your mouth.

And now the undying Worm makes no great stir,
His tight embrace chills not our luxuries,
Though the last light perfumes our bones like myrrh
And Time's beat dies.
                    Come, with your kiss renew
The day till all the old worlds die like dew.

When the green century of summer rains
Lay on the leaves, then like the rose I wept.
For I had dwelt in sorrow as the rose
In the deep heaven of her leaves lies close.
Then you, my gardener, with green fingers stroked my leaves
Till all the gold drops turned to honey. Grieves
This empire of green shade when honeyed rains
And amber blood flush all the sharp green veins
Of the rich rose?
                    So doth my rose-shaped heart
Feel the first flush of summer; love's first smart
Seemed no more sorrowful than the deep tears
The rose wept in that green and honeyed clime.

The green rains drip like the slow beat of Time
That grows within the amber blood, green veins
Of the rich rose, and in the rose-shaped heart,

—Changing the amber flesh to a clay wall.
Then comes the endless cold
At last, that is the Zero, mighty, old,
Huge as the heart, but than the worm more small—
Our final structure, the heart's ragged dress
That rose from Nothing, fell to Nothingness.

For the vast universal Night shall cover
The earth from Pole to Pole, and like a lover
Invade your heart that changed into my stone,
And I your Sisyphus. We two shall lie
Like those within the grave's eternity
And dream our arms hold the horizons deep
Where the strong suns come freshened from deep seas,
The continents beyond discoveries,
Eternal youth, and the gods' wisdom, sleep.

How should I dream that I must wake alone
With a void coffin of sad flesh and bone:—
You, with the small undying serpent's kiss,
You, the dull rumour of the dust's renown—
The polar night, a boulder rolling down
My heart, your Sisyphus, to that abyss
Where is nor light, nor dark, nor soul, nor heart to eat—
Only the dust of all the dead, the sound of passing feet.'

So winter fell, the heart shaped like the rose
Beneath the mountain of oblivion lies
With all death's nations and the centuries.
And this song ending fades like the shrill snows,
Dim as the languid moon's vast fading light
That scatters sparkles faint and dim and chill
Upon the wide leaves round my window sill
Like Aethiopia ever jeweled bright. . . .

So fading from the branches the snow sang
With a strange perfume, a melodious twang,
As if a rose should change into a ghost—
A ghost turn to a perfume on the leaves.

Metamorphosis

The coral-cold snow seemed the Parthenon—
Huge peristyle of temples that are gone—

And in the winter's Aethiopian shade—
The time of the cold heart and the world's winter—
Death seemed our only clime—
And Death our bell to chime

The passing tears among the heavy leaves
Where black as a Negress in the winter night
Is the face of Beauty in the great moon's light.

But all the nations and the centuries
And weight of Death press down upon mine eyes
In this deep-perfumed dwelling of the dead;

The dark-green country temple of the snows
Hides the porphyry bones of nymphs whence grew the rose

And dark-green dog-haired leaves of strawberries
All marked with maps of unknown lands and seas,

Among the grass that seemed like beaver's wool,
In winter, where that ruined temple's cool

Shade fell. Here, once in Spring, the dew with golden foot
Made tremble every leaf and hidden root,

41

The Sitwell family in 1901. From left, Edith, Sir George, Lady Ida, Osbert and Sacheverell.

Painting by John Singer Sargent.

mpant

An actor, director, and sometime drama teacher, Mr. Linney focuses also on the interior dramas of these lives. He concentrates on the motive power behind these spiritual reclamations. Seeing his own self-destructive father in Starns, the Bishop helps him to transfigure his life. Perceiving his former debasement enacted by the Valley's heathens, Starns helps them rejoin the human—and Christian—community. A whole series of such perceptions links disparate characters.

Characterization is one of this novel's strengths. Writing as omniscient narrator, the author endows his people and their milieu with life through vivid and sometimes poetic detail. When he writes in their voices, as an old reflective woman or a young hallucinated man, the idiom they use is as convincing as the thoughts and emotions

Painting by Charles Sibley. Courtesy Janet Nessler Gallery.
'Strong, silent and long-suffering."

Cornered in Calabria

REVOLT IN ASPROMONTE By Cor-   herd Argiro and his gentle old-

But knowing the birth of a great flower among a million
Flowers, the extinction of a far-off sun
And its many-hued perihelion and aphelion—
The extinction of a heart—all these are one.

For what should they know of lesser loves and fears
From their long aeons—or of the passing years,

And nights more dark than theirs, wherein we grope
From the more terrible abyss of hope

To soft despair . . . the nights when creeping Fear
Crumples our hearts, knowing when Age appears

Our sun, our love, will leave us more alone
Than the black mouldering rags about the bone!

Age shrinks our hearts to ape-like dust . . . that Ape
Looks through the eyes where all Death's chasms gape

Between our self and what we used to be . . .
My soul, my Lazarus, know you not me?

What gap of Death is there? What has Time done
That I should be unworthy of the Sun? . . .

Time is the worm, but Death our Sun, illumining our old
Dim-jeweled bones. Death is our winter cold

Before the rising of the sap. . . . Death's light upon the eyes
Could make each shapeless hump of clay grow wise:

The topaz, diamonds, sapphires of the bone,
That mineral in our earth's dark mine, alone

Leap to the eastern light. . . . Death-blinded eyes
See beyond wild bird-winged discoveries.

Death is the Sun's heat making all men black!
. . . O Death, the splendours die in the leaves' track . . .

All men are Aethiopian shades of thee.
The wild and glittering fleece Parthenope

Loosened, more rich than feathers of bright birds—
Though rich and thick as Aethiopian herds

Died like the wave, or early light that grew
In eastern quarries ripening precious dew.

Though lovely are the tombs of the dead nymphs
On the heroic shore, the glittering plinths

Of jacynth, hyacinthine waves profound
Sigh of the beauty out of sight and sound;

And many a golden foot that pressed the sands—
The panoply of suns on distant strands

Are only now an arena for the worm—
The golden flesh lies in the dust's frail storm

And beauty water-bright for long is laid
Deep in the empire of eternal shade;

Only the sighing waves know now the plinth
Of those deep tombs that were of hyacinth.

The myths of Earth are dead. Yet with an infinite
Wild strength the grass of spring still finds the light

45

With all the weight of earth upon its eyes
And strength, and the huge bulk of centuries.

Like Saturn's cincture, or the condensation
Of nebulae to suns, the whole spring nation

Of flowers begins . . . the lights of faith and nature.
With a hairy stalk, and with an Angel's face,
They speak of the innocent dark that gave them birth—
And of how a sun can be born from a clod of earth.

So, out of the dark, see our great Spring begins
—Our Christ, the new Song, breaking out in the fields and hedge-
            rows,
The heart of Man! O the new temper of Christ, in veins and
            branches!

He comes, our Sun, to melt the eternal ice
Of Death, the crusts of Time round the sunken soul—
Coming again in the spring of the world, clothed with the scarlet-
            coloured
Blood of our martyrdoms—the fire of spring.

Street Acrobat

TO CHARLES HENRI FORD

Upon the shore of noon, the wide azoic
Shore of diamonds where no wave comes, sprawled the nation
Of Life's rejected, with the vegetation
Of wounds that Life has made

Breaking from heart and veins. Why do they tend
With pride this flora of a new world? To what end?

But wearing the slime of Lethe's river for a dress—
Peninsulas of Misery in the Sea of Nothingness

With waves of dead rags lapping islands of the Shade,
They seem. With these for audience—
From whom you could not hope even for pence

To lay upon your eyes—
Street-corner Atlas, you support a world
Whose solar system dies in a slum room.
And what is the world you balance on your shoulder?
What fag-ends of ambition, wrecks of the heart, miasmas
From all Time's leprosies, lie there? The diamonds of the heat

Clothe you, the being diseased by Civilisation—
(With a void within the soul that has attracted
The congestion or intoxication
Of Astral Light—a gulf of diamonds—
Gyrations, revolutions, vortices
Of blinding light timed by the new pulsation!)

47

You work false miracles of anarchies
And new moralities
Designed for Bird-Men, grown with the growth of wings
From needs of Fear—
And balance high above an immeasurable abyss
Of blinding emptiness and azure vast profundities.

To the sound of ragged Madness beating his drum
Of Death in the heart, you, the atavistic, the Ape-Man,
The World-Eater, call to Darkness your last Mate
To come from her world, the phantom of yours. Then,
            Strong Man, shake
The pillars of this known world, the Palace, and Slum.

Or bear this breaking world—turn acrobat,
And execute dizzy somersaults from Real
To the Ideal—swing from desolate heavens
Of angels who seem Pharisees and Tartuffes,
Januses, gulls, and money-lenders, mediums,
In those false heavens of cloud—down to a comfortable hell—
And swing this easy world and watch it heel
Over before it fell,

To the admiration of the Lost Men nursing their wounds
And the children old in the dog's scale of years—
With only this sight for bread. . . . (Oh, seeing these,
I thought the eyes of Men
Held all the suns of the world for tears, and these were shed—
Are fallen and gone!
So dark are the inexpiable years).

But I, whose heart broke down to its central earth
And spilled its fire, its rubies, garnets, like the heat
And light from the heart of the rose,

48

Still lie immortal in the arms of Fire
Amid the ruins. The Acrobat on his tight-rope, stretched from
        beast
To God, over a vast abyss

Advances, then recedes. Or on his ladder of false light
Swings from mock heaven to real hell. And Galileo, blind,
Stares with his empty eyes on the crowds of planets and young
        roses
Beyond the arithmeticians'

Counting! O the grandeur of the instinct! The young people and
        young flowers,
Who, careless, come out in green dark,
Are numberless as the true heavens; still, in this world
    We measure by means of the old mathematicians'
Rods—or by rays of light—by the beat of Time, or the sound of
        the heart
And vibrating atoms that soon will be Man or Flower.

Said King Pompey

SAID King Pompey the emperor's ape,
Shuddering black in his temporal cape
Of dust. . . . 'The dust is everything—
The heart to love and the voice to sing,
Indianapolis
And the Acropolis,
Also the hairy wing that we
Take for a coverlet comfortably. . . .'
Said the Bishop 'The world is flat. . . .
But the see-saw crowd sent the Emperor down
To the howling dust—and up went the Clown
With his face that is filched from the new young Dead;
And the Tyrant's ghost and the Low-Man-Flea
Are emperor brothers—throw shades that are red
From the tide of blood (Red Sea, Dead Sea),
And Attila's voice or the hum of a gnat
Can usher in Eternity.'

Twelve Early Poems

I

Early Spring

THE wooden chalets of the cloud
Hang down their dull blunt ropes to shroud

Red crystal bells upon each bough
(Fruit-buds that whimper). No winds slough

Our faces, furred with cold like red
Furred buds of satyr springs, long dead!

The cold wind creaking in my blood
Seems part of it, as grain of wood;

Among the coarse goat-locks of snow
Mamzelle still drags me to and fro;

Her feet make marks like centaur hoofs
In hairy snow; her cold reproofs

Die, and her strange eyes look oblique
As the slant crystal buds that creak.

If she could think me distant, she
In the snow's goat-locks certainly

Would try to milk those teats, the buds,
Of their warm sticky milk—the cuds

Of strange long-past fruit-hairy springs—
The beginnings of first earthy things.

II

Dark Song

THE fire was furry as a bear
And the flames purr. . . .
The brown bear rambles in his chain
Captive to cruel men
Through the dark and hairy wood. . . .
The maid sighed, 'All my blood
Is animal. They thought I sat
Like a household cat;
But through the dark woods rambled I. . . .
Oh, if my blood would die!'
The fire had a bear's fur;
It heard and knew. . . .
The dark earth furry as a bear,
Grumbled too!

III

By the Lake

ACROSS the flat and the pastel snow
Two people go. . . . 'And do you remember
When last we wandered this shore?' . . . 'Ah no!

For it is cold-hearted December.'
'Dead, the leaves that like asses' ears hung on the trees
When last we wandered and squandered joy here;
Now Midas your husband will listen for these
Whispers—these tears for joy's bier.'
And as they walk, they seem tall pagodas;
And all the ropes let down from the cloud
Ring the hard cold bell-buds upon the trees—codas
Of overtones, ecstasies, grown for love's shroud.

IV

The Greengage Tree

FROM gold-mosaic'd wave
And from my fountain cave
Grew my dark-plumaged leaves all green and fountain-cold,
My minarets of gold,

Mosaic'd like the tomb,
Far in the forest gloom,
Of water-lovely Fatima in forests far away.
The gardener doth sway

The branches and doth find
(As wrinkled dark and kind
As satyrs) these with satyrs' straw beards twined
By that gold-fingered arborist the wind.

Among thick leaves the shade
Seems like a cavalcade
Or Artemus plume-helmeted from a sylvan serenade,
Or the Amazon's ambassade.

The Caliph plays a lute,
A gardener plays a flute,
Then from my feathered stem a most delightful gust, a glittering
        sea
Grows in my rich fruit.

And each bird-angel comes
To sip dark honey from my plums,
My rich green amber gums—
That make puffed feather sleeves, long feathered skirts all gold
And sticky from the dew my golden net doth hold.

V

Daphne

HEAT of the sun that maketh all men black—
They are but Aethiopian shades of thee—
Pour down upon this wild and glittering fleece
That is more rich than feathers of bright birds,
The ripening gems, the drops of the still night.
I parch for that still shade; my heat of love
That parched those ripening gems hath withered me.

Come with the African pomp and train of waves—
Give me your darkness, my immortal shade,
Beside the water-wells my heart hath known.
The shepherds hairy-rough as satyrs come,
Bring up their fleeces that are water-full
With freshness clear as precious gums of trees
Where weep the incense-trees from some deep smart:
So the fresh water from your fleece flows in
To fill with richness all my desert heart.

54

VI

The Soldan's Song

(FROM 'THE SLEEPING BEAUTY')

WHEN green as a river was the barley,
Green as a river the rye,
I waded deep and began to parley
With a youth whom I heard sigh.
'I seek,' said he, 'a lovely lady,
A nymph as bright as a queen,
Like a tree that drips with pearls her shady
Locks of hair were seen;
And all the rivers became her flocks,
Though their wool you cannot shear,
Because of the love of her flowing locks.
The kingly sun like a swain
Came strong, unheeding of her scorn,
Wading in deeps where she has lain,
Sleeping upon her river lawn
And chasing her starry satyr train.
She fled, and changed into a tree—
That lovely fair-haired lady. . . .
And now I seek through the sere summer
Where no trees are shady.'

VII

Song of the Man from the Far Country

'Rose and Alice,
Oh, the pretty lassies,
With their mouths like a calice
And their hair a golden palace—
Through my heart like a lovely wind they blow.

Though I am black and not comely,
Though I am black as the darkest trees,
I have swarms of gold that will fly like honey-bees,
By the rivers of the sun I will feed my words
Until they skip like those fleecèd lambs
The waterfalls, and the rivers (horned rams);
Then for all my darkness I shall be
The peacefulness of a lovely tree—
A tree wherein the golden birds
Are singing in the darkest branches, O!'

VIII

The Governante's Song

(FROM 'THE SLEEPING BEAUTY')

'Look not on the infinite wave,
Dream not of the siren cave,
Nor hear the cold wind in the tree
Sigh of worlds we cannot see.'
(She sings.)

'The hot muscatelle
Siesta time fell,
And the Spanish belle
Looked out through the shutters.

Under the eglantine
Thorny and lean
A shadow was playing a mandoline, mutters

Only this: "Wave
Your fan . . . siren cave
Never was cold as the wind from the grave." '

The governante
Came walking andante—
Sailed like a brigantine, black of brow.

And the falconette
Who danced a ballette
Sang on the pretty, the brunette bough:

'The ambassade
Of shadows invade
Death's most ultimate, peaceful shade. . . .
Lovely lady, where are you now?'

IX

Through Gilded Trellises

(FROM 'THE SLEEPING BEAUTY')

THROUGH gilded trellises
Of the heat, Dolores,
Inez, Manuccia,
Isabel, Lucia,
Mock Time that flies.
'Lovely bird, will you stay and sing,
Flirting your sheenèd wing—
Peck with your beak, and cling
To our balconies?'
They flirt their fans, flaunting—
'O silence, enchanting
As music!' then slanting
Their eyes,
Like gilded or emerald grapes,
They take mantillas, capes,
Hiding their simian shapes.
Sighs
Each lady, 'Our spadille
Is done! . . . Dance the quadrille
From Hell's towers to Seville:
Surprise
Their siesta!' Dolores
Said. Through gilded trellises
Of the heat, spangles
Pelt down through the tangles
Of bell-flowers; each dangles
Her castenets, shutters
Fall while the heat mutters,

With sounds like a mandoline
Or tinkled tambourine. . . .
'Ladies, Time dies!'

X

Waltz

DAISY and Lily,
Lazy and silly,
Walk by the shore of the wan grassy sea—
Talking once more 'neath a swan-bosomed tree.
Rose castles,
Tourelles,
Those bustles
Where swells
Each foam-bell of ermine,
They roam and determine
What fashions have been and what fashions will be—
What tartan leaves born,
What crinolines worn.
By Queen Thetis,
Pelisses
Of tarlatine blue
Like the thin plaided leaves that the castle crags grew,
Or velours d'Afrande:
On the water-gods' land
Her hair seemed gold trees on the honey-cell sand
When the thickest gold spangles on deep waters seen
Were like twanging guitar and like cold mandoline,
And the nymphs of great caves
With hair like gold waves

Of Venus, wore tarlatine.
Louise and Charlottine
(Boreas' daughters)
And the nymphs of deep waters,
The nymph Taglioni, Grisi the ondine,
Wore plaided Victoria and thin Clementine
Like the crinolined waterfalls;
Wood-nymphs wore bonnets, shawls;
Elegant parasols
Floating were seen.
The Amazons wear balzarine of jonquille
Beside the blond lace of a deep-falling rill.
Through glades like a nun
They run from and shun
The enormous and gold-rayed rustling sun.
And the nymphs of the fountains
Descend from the mountains
Like elegant willows
On their deep barouche pillows
In cashmere Alvandar, barège Isabelle,
Like bells of bright water from clearest woodwell.
Our élégantes favouring bonnets of blond,
The stars in their apiaries,
Sylphs in their aviaries,
Seeing them, spangle these, and the sylphs fond
From their aviaries fanned
With each long fluid hand
The manteaux espagnoles,
Mimic the waterfalls
Over the long and the light summer land.

So Daisy and Lily,
Lazy and silly,

Walk by the shore of the wan grassy sea,
Talking once more 'neath a swan-bosomed tree.
Rose castles,
Tourelles,
Those bustles!
Mourelles
Of the shade in their train follow.
Ladies, how vain—hollow—
Gone is the sweet swallow—
Gone, Philomel!

XI

The Wind's Bastinado

THE wind's bastinado
Whipt on the calico
Skin of the Macaroon
And the black Picaroon
Beneath the galloon
Of the midnight sky.
Came the great Soldan
In his sedan
Floating his fan—
Saw what the sly
Shadow's cocoon
In the barracoon
Held. Out they fly.
'This melon,
Sir Mammon,
Comes out of Babylon:
Buy for a patacoon—
Sir, you must buy!'

61

Said Il Magnifico
Pulling a fico—
With a stoccado
And a gambado,
Making a wry
Face: 'This corraceous
Round orchidaceous
Laceous porraceous
Fruit is a lie!
It is my friend King Pharaoh's head
That nodding blew out of the Pyramid. . . .'
The tree's small corinths
Were hard as jacinths,
For it is winter and cold winds sigh. . . .
No nightingale
In her farthingale
Of bunchèd leaves let her singing die. . . .

XII

The Drum

(THE NARRATIVE OF THE DEMON OF TEDWORTH)

In HIS tall senatorial
Black and manorial
House where decoy-duck
Dust doth clack—
Clatter and quack
To a shadow black—
Said the musty Justice Monpesson:
'What is that dark stark beating drum

That we hear rolling like the sea?'
'It is a beggar with a pass
Signed by you.' 'I signed not one.'
They took the ragged drum that we
Once heard rolling like the sea;
In the house of the Justice it must lie
And usher in Eternity.

Is it black night?
Black as Hecate howls a star
Wolfishly, and whined
The wind from very far.

In the pomp of the Monpesson house is one
Candle that lolls like the midnight sun,
Or the coral comb of a cock; . . . it rocks. . . .
Only the goatish snow's locks
Watch the candles lit by fright
One by one through the black night.

Through the kitchen there runs a hare—
Whinnying, whines like grass, the air;
It passes; now is standing there
A lovely lady . . . see her eyes—
Black angels in a heavenly place,
Her shady locks and her dangerous grace.

'I thought I saw the wicked old witch in
The richest gallipot in the kitchen!'
A lolloping galloping candle confesses.
'Outside in the passage are wildernesses
Of darkness rustling like witches' dresses.'

Out go the candles one by one
Hearing the rolling of a drum!

What is the march we hear groan
As the hoofèd sound of a drum marched on
With a pang like darkness, with a clang
Blacker than an orang-outang?
'Heliogabalus is alone—
Only his bones to play upon!'

The mocking money in the pockets
Then turned black . . . now caws
The fire . . . outside, one scratched the door
As with iron claws—

Scratching under the children's bed
And up the trembling stairs. . . . 'Long dead'
Moaned the water black as crape.
Over the snow the wintry moon,
Limp as henbane, or herb-paris,
Spotted the bare trees; and soon,

Whinnying, neighed the maned blue wind,
Turning the burning milk to snow,
Whining, it shied down the corridor,
Over the floor I heard it go
Where the drum rolls up the stair, nor tarries.

The Poet Laments the Coming of
Old Age

I SEE the children running out of school;
They are taught that Goodness means a blinding hood
Or is heaped by Time like the hump on an agèd back,
And that Evil can be cast like an old rag
And Wisdom caught like a hare and held in the golden sack
Of the heart. . . . But I am one who must bring back sight to the
      blind.

Yet there was a planet dancing in my mind
With a gold seed of Folly . . . long ago. . . .
And where is that grain of Folly? . . . with the hare-wild wind
Of my spring it has gone from one who must bring back sight to
      the blind.

For I, the fool, was once like the philosopher
Sun who laughs at evil and at good:
I saw great things mirrored in littleness,
Who now see only that great Venus wears Time's filthy dress—
A toothless crone who once had the Lion's mouth.

The Gold Appearances from Nothing rise
In sleep, by day . . . two thousand years ago
There was a man who had the Lion's leap,
Like the Sun's, to take the worlds and loves he would,
But (laughed the philosopher Sun, and I, the fool)

Great golden Alexander and his thunder-store
Are now no more
Than the armoured knight who buzzed on the windowpane
And the first drops of rain.

He lies in sleep. . . . But still beneath a thatch
Of hair like sunburnt grass, the thieving sweet thoughts move
Toward the honey-hive. . . . And another sweet-tooth Alexander
    runs
Out of the giant shade that is his school
To take the dark knight's world, the honeycomb.

The Sun's simulacrum, the gold-sinewed man
Lies under a hump of grass, as once I thought to wear
With patience, Goodness like a hump on my agèd back.
. . . But Goodness grew not with age, although the heart must
    bear
The weight of all Time's filth, and Wisdom is not a hare in the
    golden sack

Of the heart. . . . It can never be caught. Though I bring back
    sight to the blind,
My seed of Folly has gone, that could teach me to bear
That the gold-sinewed body that had the blood of all the earth in
    its veins,
Has changed to an old rag of the outworn world;
And the great heart that the first Morning made
Should wear all Time's destruction for a dress.

Spring Morning

TO KENNETH AND JANE CLARK

AFTER the thunders of night-wandering Zagreus
The unseen Suns were singing, where day-long, laughter,
The Janus-face, turned black and terrible, as if lightning
Struck it among bright vine-tips.

The night dews and the night still lie
In the almandine violet heart of deepest shade;
The dancing seas of delight lie on young leaves,

Young heart upon young heart. O night of ferment in the heart
   and under earth!
The sapphire tears fallen from the heavens will reach
The fissures in the heart and rock, too deep
And narrow for the grandeur of the Sun.
But what has the Night ripened?
What depths in that sapphiric mine, our body's earth?

Then rose our Sun. . . . He shouts through all creation. His gold
   fires
Shake from each heaven to heaven . . . and at his kiss
From hemisphere to hemisphere the rising fires in all the hearts
   and homes of Men
Respond; and I, still wrapped in darkness, cry
With the voice of all those rolling fires 'Hail to the great Sun and
   to the Sun in the heart of Man!'
—Till the last fire fall in the last abyss.

In the violent Spring, amid the thunders of the sap and the blood
        in the heart
The Sun answers the cries
From the frost that shines like fire or the dust of Venus in the time
Of the rites of the Croconides—
Fertilising the saffron.

                          And the sound of the earth's desire
Reaches the bones of the Lion, the Horse, the Man; under their
        great Death
Like Spring, they feel the great saps rise—
The power of the Sun.

And in the House of Gold, the House of the Dead,
The bones of ancient lions shake like fire.
The dead men, the gold forms to whom all growth belongs,

Hear the shout of the God in the Gold Rain and its marriage with
        the earth—
And the crocus, whose race has sprung from gold, is born again.

Then the King who is part of the saffronic dust
—He of the gold sinews, withered now—
Sighed 'Darkness clasps the root, the gold, the heart.

But the gold is brother to the root! Will it learn to grow
Through the long ages till it change to plant? . . .
Will the Sun kiss its long hair? And will my heart
Be changed to gold? . . . Ah, when shall I know

Again the kiss outburning all the fires of the crocus?
When from gold lips that are long since dust shall I light my Sun?'

Then from the wide pale lips of the dust came the great sound
Of the Ritual Laughter
At the impiety of Death, the sacrilege.

'For,' said the great dust to the small serpent that devours
The saffronic dust of Venus, the spring hours. . . .
'See how the Sun comes with his gold love to kiss our baseness.

He pities the small worm and its lipless mouthing
At the earth's bosom like a babe at its mother's breast:
From the mouthing of the small worm, when the world began
Arose the speech, arose the kiss of Man.

And the beast who shares with Man Time and the beat of the heart,
And the great gold beasts who shake their manes through all high
        heaven, to him are one.'

The Sun comes to the saps of Reason . . . sighs all sighs
And suffers all ambitions . . . cries
To the subterranean fires in Croesus' heart, the unborn wheat
'Your gold must grow that the starved may eat!'

And from the Chaos of our Nature, the brute gold
In every seam and vein of earth roars to the Sun.

So Day begins . . . and the course of the Sun is followed by the
        solar heroes,
The men of common earth, of the common task;
With their gold sinews lifting the world, they offer to the Morning

The palms of all their martyrdoms and grandeurs,
The dews of Death. . . . And in the roads I see the common dust
Change to an Archangel,
Beneath the Sun's gold breath.

And I in answer raise
My arms and my long hands like the young vine-boughs
With the gold blood running and sunning to the tips of the grape-
        shaped finger-ends—
Raise them in praise.

My blood is one with the young vines—part of the earth: I shout
        from my planet, quickening
As the great Sun in the void firmament,
My heart that gives life to my earth like water and the hot gold
Flames of the laughing Sun, grown strong as these.

The Song of the Cold

TO NATASHA LITVIN

HUGE is the sun of amethysts and rubies,
And in the purple perfumes of the polar sun
And homeless cold they wander.
But winter is the time for comfort, and for friendship,
For warmth and food—
And a talk beside a fire like the Midnight Sun—
A glowing heart of amber and of musk. Time to forget
The falling night of the world and heart, the polar chaos
That separates us each from each. It is no time to roam
Along the pavements wide and cold as Hell's huge polar street,
Drifting along the city like the wind
Blowing aimlessly, and with no home
To rest in, only famine for a heart—
While Time means nothing to one, as to the wind
Who only cares for ending and beginning.

Here in the fashionable quarters of the city
Cold as the universal blackness of Hell's day
The two opposing brotherhoods are swept
Down the black marble pavements, Lethe's river.
First come the worlds of Misery, the small and tall Rag-Castles,
Shut off from every other. These have no name,
Nor friend to utter it . . . these of the extinct faces
Are a lost civilisation, and have no possession
But the night and day, those centuries of cold.
Even their tears are changed now to the old
Eternal nights of ice round the loveless head
Of these who are lone and sexless as the Dead.

71

Dives of the Paleocrystic heart, behold
These who were once your brothers. Hear their voices
Hoarsened by want to the rusty voice of the tiger, no more crying
The death of the soul, but lamenting their destitution.
What life, what solar system of the heart
Could bring a restitution
To these who die of the cold?
                    Some keep their youthful graces,
Yet in their winding-sheets of rags seem early
Made ready for the grave. . . . Worn to the bone by their famine
As if by the lusts that the poor Dead have known,
Who now are cold for ever. . . . Those who are old
Seem humbler, lean their mouths to the earth as if to crop
The kind earth's growth—for this is the Cainozoic period
When we must learn to walk with the gait of the Ape and Tiger:
The warmth of the heart is dead, or has changed to the world's
            fever—
And love is but masked murder, the lust for possession,
The hunger of the Ape, or the confession
Of the last fear, the wish to multiply
Their image, of a race on Oblivion's brink.

Lazarus, weep for those who have known the lesser deaths, O
            think
How we should pity the High Priests of the god of this world,
            the saints of Mammon,
The cult of gold! For see how these, too, ache with the cold
From the polar wastes of the heart. . . . See all they have given
Their god! Are not their veins grown ivy-old,
And have they not eaten their own hearts and lives in their famine?

Their huge Arithmetic is but the endless
Repetition of Zero—the unlimited,

Eternal. Even the beat of the heart and the pulse is changed
      to this:
The counting of small deaths, the repetition
Of Nothing, endless positing and suppression of Nothing. . . .
      So they live
And die of inanition. . . .

             The miser Foscue
Weaving his own death and sinking like a spider
To vaults and depths that held his gold, that sun,
Was walled in that grave by the rotting hand of the dust, by a
      trap-door falling.
Do the enormous rays of that Sun now warm his blood, the appal-
      ling
Empty gulf of his veins—or fertilise
His flesh, that continent of dryness? . . . Yellow, cold,
And crumbling as his gold,
Deserted by the god of this world, a Gold Man like a terrible Sun,
A Mummy with a Lion's mane,
He sits in this desert where no sound of wave shall come,
And Time's sands are of gold, filling his ears and eyes,
And he who has grown the talons of the Lion
Has devoured the flesh of his own hands and heart in his pain.

Pity these hopeless acolytes . . . the vain
Prudence that emulates the wisdom of the Spider
Who spins but for herself—a world of Hunger
Constructed for the needs of Hunger. . . . Soon
Their blankets will be thinner than her thread:
When comes the Night when they have only gold
For flesh, for warmth, for sheet—
O who would not pity these,
Grown fleshless, too, as those who starve and freeze!

Now falls the Night on Lazarus and Dives—
Those who were brothers, those who shared the pain
Of birth, and lusts, and the daily lesser deaths,
The beat of the dying heart, the careful breaths:
'You are so worn to the bone, I thought you were Death, my
        brother—
Death who will warm my heart.' 'Have you too known the cold?
Give me your hand to warm me. I am no more alone.
There was a sun that shone
On all alike, but the cold in the heart of Man
Has slain it. Where is it gone?'

So in the great Night that comes like love, so small they lie
As when they lay close to their mother's breast,
Naked and bare in their mortality.

Soon comes the Night when those who were never loved
Shall know the small immortal serpent's kiss
And turn to dust as lover turns to lover. . . .
Then all shall know the cold's equality. . . .
Young Beauty, bright as the tips of the budding vine,
You with the gold Appearances from Nothing rise
In the spring wind, and but for a moment shine.

Dust are the temples that were bright as heat . . .
And, perfumed nosegay brought for noseless Death,
Your brightest myrrh can not perfume his breath!

That old rag-picker blown along the street
Was once great Venus. But now Age unkind
Has shrunken her so feeble and so small—
Weak as a babe. And she who gave the Lion's kiss
Has now all Time's gap for her piteous mouth.

74

What lullaby will Death sing, seeing this
Small babe? And she of the golden feet,
To what love does she haste? After these centuries
The sun will be her only kiss—now she is blackened, shrunken, old
As the small worm—her kiss, like his, grown cold.

In the nights of spring, the inner leaf of the heart
Feels warm, and we will pray for the eternal cold
Of those who are only warmed by the sins of the world—
And those whose nights were violent like the buds
And roots of spring, but like the spring, grew old.
Their hearts are tombs on the heroic shore,
That were of iris, diamond, hyacinth,
And now are patterned only by Time's wave . . . the glittering
        plinth
Is crumbling. . . . But the great sins and fires break out of me
Like the terrible leaves from the bough in the violent spring. . . .
I am a walking fire, I am all leaves—
I will cry to the Spring to give me the birds' and the serpents'
        speech
That I may weep for those who die of the cold—
The ultimate cold within the heart of Man.

The Coat of Fire

AMID the thunders of the falling Dark
In the Tartarean darkness of the fog
I walk, a Pillar of Fire,
On pavements of black marble, hard
And wide as the long boulevard
Of Hell . . . I, in whose veins the Furies wave
Their long fires, pass where purgatories, heavens, hells, and worlds
Wrought by illusion, hide in the human breast
And tear the enclosing heart. . . . And the snow fell
(Thin flakes of ash from Gomorrah) on blind faces
Turned to the heedless sky. . . . A dress has the sound
Of Reality, reverberates like thunder.
And ghosts of aeons and of equinoxes
(Of moments that seemed aeons, and long partings)
Take on the forms of fashionable women
With veils that hide a new Catastrophe, and under
Is the fall of a world that was a heart. Some doomed to descend
Through all the hells and change into the Dog
Without its faithfulness, the Crocodile
Without its watchfulness, and then to Pampean mud.
In the circles of the city's hells beneath the fog
These bear, to light them, in the human breast,
The yellow dull light from the raging human dust,
The dull blue light from the brutes, light red as rust
Of blood from eyeless weeping ghosts, light black as smoke
From hell. And those breasts bear
No other light. . . . They circle in the snow
Where in the dust the apterous

Fates turned insects whisper 'Now abandon
Man the annelida. Let all be wingless
That hangs between the Abyss and Abaddon.
The Catastrophes with veils and trains drift by,
And I to my heart, disastrous comet, cry
'Red heart, my Lucifer! How fallen art thou!
And lightless, I!'
The dresses sweep the dust of mortality
And roll the burden of Atlas' woe changed to a stone
Up to the benches where the beggars sway,
Their souls alone as on the Judgment Day
In their Valley of the Myriad Dry Bones under world-tall houses.
Then with a noise, as if in the thunders of the Dark
All sins, griefs, aberrations of the world rolled to confess,
Those myriad Dry Bones rose to testify:

'See her, the Pillar of Fire!
                                   The aeons of Cold
And all the deaths that Adam has endured
Since the first death, can not outfreeze our night!
And where is the fire of love that will warm our hands?
There is only this conflagration
Of all the sins of the world! To the dust's busyness
She speaks of the annihilation
Of every form of dust, burned down to Nothingness!
To the small lovers, of a kiss that seems the red
Lightning of Comets firing worlds—and of a Night
That shall outburn all nights that lovers know—
The last red Night before the Judgment Day!
O Pillar of Flame, that drifts across the world to Nowhere!
The eyes are seas of fire! All forms, all sights,
And all sensations are on fire! The storms
Of blood, a whirlpool of the flame! the ears, all sounds
Of all the world, a universe of fire! all smells, a ravening

77

Raging cyclone of wild fire! The nose, burned quite away!
The tongue is on fire, all tastes on fire, the mind
Is red as noon upon the Judgment Day!
The tears are rolling, falling worlds of fire!
With what are these on fire? With passion, hate,
Infatuation, and old age, and death,
With sorrow, longing, and with labouring breath,
And with despair and life are these on fire!
With the illusions of the world, the flames of lust,
And raging red desire!
A Pillar of Fire is she in the empty dust,
And will not change those fires into warmth for our hands'
Said the beggars, lolling and rocking
The heedless world upon a heaving shoulder.

Gold Coast Customs

TO HELEN ROOTHAM

In Ashantee, a hundred years ago, the death of any rich or important person was followed by several days of national ceremonies, during which the utmost licence prevailed, and slaves and poor persons were killed that the bones of the deceased might be washed with human blood. These ceremonies were called Customs.

ONE fantee wave
Is grave and tall
As brave Ashantee's
Thick mud wall.
Munza rattles his bones in the dust,
Lurking in murk because he must.

Striped black and white
Is the squealing light;
The dust brays white in the market place,
Dead powder spread on a black skull's face.

Like monkey-skin
Is the sea—one sin
Like a weasel is nailed to bleach on the rocks
Where the eyeless mud screeched fawning, mocks

At a Negro that wipes
His knife . . . dug there,
A bugbear bellowing
Bone dared rear—
A bugbear bone that bellows white
As the ventriloquist sound of light,

It rears at his headdress of felted black hair
The one humanity clinging there—
His eyeless face whitened like black and white bones
And his beard of rusty
Brown grass cones.

Hard blue and white
Cowrie shells (the light
Grown hard) outline
The leopard-skin musty
Leaves that shine
With an animal smell both thick and fusty.

One house like a rat-skin
Mask flaps fleet
In the sailor's tall
Ventriloquist street
Where the rag houses flap—
Hiding a gap,

Here, tier on tier
Like a black box rear
In the flapping slum
Beside Death's docks.
I did not know this meaner Death
Meant this: that the bunches of nerves still dance
And caper among these slums, and prance.

'Mariners, put your bones to bed!'
But at Lady Bamburgher's parties each head,
Grinning, knew it had left its bones
In the mud with the white skulls . . . only the grin
Is left, strings of nerves, and the drum-taut skin.

When the sun in the empty
Sky is high
In his dirty brown and white
Bird-skin dress—
He hangs like a skull
With a yellow dull
Face made of clay
(Where tainted, painted, the plague-spots bray)
To hide where the real face rotted away.
So our worm-skin and paper masks still keep,
Above the rotting bones they hide,
The marks of the Plague whereof we died:
The belief,
The grief,
The love,
Or the grin
Of the shapeless worm-soft unshaping Sin—
Unshaping till no more the beat of the blood
Can raise up the body from endless mud
Though the hell-fires, cold
As the worm, and old,
Are painted upon each unshaped form—
No more man, woman, or beast to see—
But the universal devouring Worm.

When the sun of dawn looks down on the shrunken
Heads, drums of skin, and the dead men drunken,
I only know one half of my heart
Lies in that terrible coffin of stone,
My body that stalks through the slum alone.
And that half of my heart
That is in your breast
You gave for meat

In the sailor's street
To the rat that had only my bones to eat.

But those hardened hearts
That roll and sprawl,
In a cowl of foul blind monkey-skin,
Lest the whips of the light crash roaring in—
Those hearts that roll
Down the phantom street,
They have for their beat
The cannibal drums
And the cries of the slums,
And the Bamburgher parties—they have them all!

One high house flaps . . . taps
Light's skin drum—
Monkey-like shrunk
On all fours now come
The parties' sick ghosts, each hunting himself—
Black gaps beneath an ape's thick pelt.

Chasing a rat,
Their soul's ghost fat
Through the Negro swamp,
Slum hovel's cramp,
Of Lady Bamburgher's parties above
With the latest grin, and the latest love,
And the latest game:
To show the shame
Of the rat-fat soul to the grinning day
With even the rat-skin flayed away.

Now, a thick cloud floating
Low o'er the lake,

Millions of flies
Begin to awake,
With the animation
Of smart conversation:
From Bedlam's madness the thick gadflies
Seek for the broken statue's eyes.

Where the mud and the murk
Whispering lurk:
'From me arises everything,
The Negro's louse,
The armadillo,
Munza's bone and his peccadillo.'—

Where flaps degraded
The black and sated
Slack macerated
And antiquated
Beckoning Negress
Nun of the shade,
And the rickety houses
Rock and rot,
Lady Bamburgher airs
That foul plague-spot,
Her romantic heart.
From the cannibal mart,
That smart Plague-cart,
Lady Bamburgher rolls where the foul news-sheet
And the shambles for souls are set in the street.

And stuck in front
Of this world-tall Worm,
Stuck in front
Of this world's confession—

83

Like something rolled
Before a procession,
Is the face, a flimsy worm-skin thing
That someone has raked
From the low plague-pit
As a figurehead
For Corruption dead,
And a mask for the universal Worm.

Her ape-skin yellow
Tails of hair
Clung about her bone-white bare
Eyeless mask that cackled there:

The Worm's mask hid
Her eyeless mud,
Her shapeless love,
The plot to escape
From the God-ordained shape

And her soul, the cannibal
Amazon's mart,
Where in squealing light
And clotted black night
On the monkey-skin black and white striped dust they
Cackle and bray to the murdered day.

And the Amazon queen
With a bone-black face
Wears a mask with an ape-skin beard; she grinds
Her male child's bones in a mortar, binds
Him for food, and the people buy. For this,

Hidden behind
The Worm's mask, grown

White as a bone
Where eyeholes rot wide
And are painted for sight,
And the little mouth red as a dead Plague-spot
On that white mask painted to hide Death's rot,

For this painted Plague-cart's
Heart, for this
Slime of the Worm that paints her kiss
And the dead men's bones round her throat and wrist,
The half of my heart that lay in your breast
Has fallen away
To rot and bray
With the painted mud through the eyeless day.

The dust of all the dead can blow
Backwards and forwards, to and fro,
To cover the half of my heart with death's rot,
Yet the dust of that other half comes not
To this coffin of stone that stalks through the slum,
Though love to you now is the deaf Worm's lust
That, cloven in halves, will re-unite
Foulness to deadness in the dust
And chaos of the enormous night.

How far is our innocent paradise,
The blue-striped sand,
Bull-bellowing band
Of waves, and the great gold suns made wise
By the dead days and the horizons grand!

Can a planet tease
With its great gold train,
Walking beside the pompous main—

That great gold planet the heat of the Sun
Where we saw black Shadow, a black man, run,
So a Negress dare
Wear long gold hair?
The Negress Dorothy one sees
Beside the caverns and the trees
Where her parasol
Throws a shadow tall
As a waterfall—
The Negress Dorothy still feels
The great gold planet tease her brain.

And dreaming deep within her blood
Lay Africa like the dark in the wood;
For Africa is the unhistorical,
Unremembering, unrhetorical,
Undeveloped spirit involved
In the conditions of nature—Man,
That black image of stone, hath delved
On the threshold where history began.

Now under the cannibal
Sun is spread
The black rhinoceros-hide of the mud
For endlessness and timelessness . . . dead
Grass creaks like a carrion-bird's voice, rattles,
Squeaks like a wooden shuttle. Battles
Have worn this deserted skeleton black
As empty chain armour . . . lazily back
With only the half of its heart it lies
With the giggling mud devouring its eyes;
Naught left to fight
But the black clotted night
In its heart, and ventriloquist squealing light.

But lying beneath the giggling mud
I thought there was something living, the bray
Of the eyeless mud can not betray—
Though it is buried beneath black bones
Of the fetiches screeching like overtones
Of the light, as they feel the slaves' spilt blood.

In tiers like a box
Beside the docks
The Negro prays,
The Negro knocks.
'Is anyone there?'
His mumblings tear
Nothing but paper walls, and the blare
Of the gaping capering empty air.
The cannibal drums still roll in the mud
To the bones of the king's mother laved in blood
And the trophies with long black hair, shrunken heads
That, drunken, shrunk upon tumbled beds.

The Negro rolls
His red eyeballs,
Prostrates himself.
The Negro sprawls:
His God is but a flat black stone
Upright upon a squeaking bone.

The Negro's dull
Red eyeballs roll . . .
The immortality of the soul
Is but black ghosts that squeak through the hole
That once seemed eyes in Munza's skull.

This is his god:
The cannibal sun

On bones that played
For evermore,
And the dusty roar
Of the ancient Dead,
And the squealing rat,
The soul's ghost fat.

But Lady Bamburgher's Shrunken Head,
Slum hovel, is full of the rat-eaten bones
Of a fashionable god that lived not
Ever, but still has bones to rot:
A bloodless and an unborn thing
That cannot wake, yet cannot sleep,
That makes no sound, that cannot weep,
That hears all, bears all, cannot move—
It is buried so deep
Like a shameful thing
In that plague-spot heart, Death's last dust-heap.

.   .   .   .

A tall house flaps
In the canvas street,
Down in the wineshop
The Amazons meet

With the tall abbess
Of the shade. . . .
A ghost in a gown
Like a stiff brigade

Watches the sailor
With a guitar
Lure the wind
From the islands far.

O far horizons and bright blue wine
And majesty of the seas that shine,
Bull-bellowing waves that ever fall
Round the godlike feet and the goddess tall!

A great yellow flower
With the silence shy
To the wind from the islands
Sighs 'I die.'

At the foot of the steps
Like the navy-blue ghost
Of a coiling Negro,
In dock slums lost,

(The ghost haunting steamers
And cocktail bars,
Card-sharpers, schemers,
And Pullman cars)

A ripple rose
With mud at its root
And weeping kissed
A statue's foot.

In the sailor's tall
Ventriloquist street
The calico dummies
Flap and meet:
Calculate: 'Sally, go
Pick up a sailor.'
Behind that façade
The worm is a jailer.

'I cannot stiffen . . . I left my bones
Down in the street: no overtones
Of the murdered light can join my dust
To my black bones pressed in the House of Lust.
Only my feet still walk in the street;
But where is my heart and its empty beat?

"Starved silly Sally, why dilly and dally?"
The dummies said when I was a girl.
The rat deserts a room that is bare,
But Want, a cruel rat gnawing there,
Ate to the heart, all else was gone,
Nothing remained but Want alone.
So now I'm a gay girl, a calico dummy,
With nothing left alive but my feet
That walk up and down in the Sailor's Street.

Behind the bawdy hovels like hoardings
Where harridans peer from the grovelling boarding
House, the lunatic
Wind still shakes
My empty rag-body, nothing wakes;
The wind, like a lunatic in a fouled
Nightgown, whipped those rags and howled.

Once I saw it come
Through the canvas slum,
Rattle and beat what seemed a drum,
Rattle and beat it with a bone.
O Christ, that bone was dead, alone!
Christ, Who will speak to such ragged Dead
As me! I am dead, alone and bare,
They expose me still to the grinning air,

I shall never gather my bones and my dust
Together (so changed and scattered, lost . . .)
So I can be decently buried!
What is that whimpering like a child
That this mad ghost beats like a drum in the air?
The heart of Sal
That once was a girl
And now is a calico thing to loll
Over the easy steps of the slum
Waiting for something dead to come.'

From Rotten Alley and Booble Street,
The beggars crawl to starve near the meat
Of the reeling appalling cannibal mart,
And Lady Bamburgher, smart Plague-cart.
Red rag face and a cough that tears,
They creep through the mud of the docks from their lairs;
And when the dog-whining dawn light
Nosed for their hearts, whined in fright,
With a sly high animal
Whimpering, half-frightened call
To worlds outside our consciousness,
It finds no heart within their dress.
The Rat has eaten
That and beaten
Hope and love and memory,
At last, and even the will to die.
But what is the loss? For you cannot sell
The heart to those that have none for Hell
To fatten on . . . or that cheap machine,
And its beat would make springs for the dancing feet
Of Lady Bamburgher down in the street
Of her dogs that nose out each other's sin,
And grin, and whine, and roll therein.

Against the Sea-wall are painted signs
'Here for a shilling a sailor dines.'
Each Rag-and-Bone
Is propped up tall
(Lest in death it fall)
Against the Sea-wall.
Their empty mouths are sewed up whole
Lest from hunger they gape and cough up their soul.
The arms of one are stretched out wide. . . .
How long, since our Christ was crucified?

Rich man Judas,
Brother Cain,
The rich men are your worms that gain
The air through seething from your brain;
Judas, mouldering in your old
Coffin body, still undying
As the Worm, where you are lying
With no flesh for warmth, but gold
For flesh, for warmth, for sheet;
Now you are fleshless, too, as these
That starve and freeze,
Is your gold hard as Hell's huge polar street,
Is the universal blackness of Hell's day so cold?

When, creeping over
The Sailor's Street
Where the houses like rat-skin
Masks flap, meet
Never across the murdered bone
Of the sailor, the whining overtone
Of dawn sounds, slaves
Rise from their graves,

Where in the corpse-sheet night they lay
Forgetting the mutilating day,
Like the unborn child in its innocent sleep.
Ah, Christ! the murdered light must weep—
(Christ that takest away the sin
Of the world, and the rich man's bone-dead grin)
The light must weep
Seeing that sleep
And those slaves rise up in their death-chains, part
The light from the eyes,
The hands from the heart,
Since their hearts are flesh for the tall
And sprawling
Reeling appalling
Cannibal mart,
But their hands and head
Are machines to breed
Gold for the old and the greedy Dead.

I have seen the murdered God look through the eyes
Of the drunkard's smirched
Mask as he lurched
O'er the half of my heart that lies in the street
'Neath the dancing fleas and the foul news-sheet.

Where (a black gap flapping,
A white skin drum)
The cannibal houses
Watch this come—
Lady Bamburgher's party; for the plan
Is a prize for those that on all fours ran
Through the rotting slum
Till those who come

Could never guess from the mud-covered shapes
Which are the rich or the mired dire apes,
As they run where the souls, dirty paper, are blown
In the hour before dawn, through this long hell of stone.

Perhaps if I, too, lie down in the mud,
Beneath tumbrils rolling
And mad skulls galloping
Far from their bunches of nerves that dance
And caper among these slums and prance,
Beneath the noise of that hell that rolls
I shall forget the shrunken souls
The eyeless mud squealing 'God is dead,'
Starved men (bags of wind) and the harlot's tread,
The heaven turned into monkey-hide
By Lady Bamburgher's dancing fleas,
Her rotting parties and death-slack ease,
And the dead men drunken
(The only tide)
Blown up and down
And tossed through the town
Over the half of my heart that lies
Deep down, in this meaner Death, with cries.

The leaves of black hippopotamus-hide
Black as the mud
Cover the blood
And the rotting world. Do we smell and see

The sick thick smoke from London burning,
Gomorrah turning
Like worms in the grave,
The Bedlam daylight's murderous roar,
Those pillars of fire the drunkard and whore,

Dirty souls boiled in cannibal cookshops to paper
To make into newspapers, flags? . . . They caper
Like gaping apes. Foul fires we see,
For Bedlam awakes to reality.

The drunkard burning,
The skin drums galloping,
In their long march still parched for the sky,
The Rotten Alleys where beggars groan
And the beggar and his dog share a bone;
The rich man Cain that hides within
His lumbering palaces where Sin
Through the eyeless holes of Day peers in,
The murdered heart that all night turns
From small machine to shapeless Worm
With hate, and like Gomorrah burns—
These put the eyes of Heaven out,
These raise all Hell's throats to a shout,
These break my heart's walls toppling in,
And like a universal sea
The nations of the Dead crowd in.

Bahunda, Banbangala, Barumbe, Bonge,
And London fall . . . rolling human skin drums
Surrounded by long black hair, I hear
Their stones that fall,
Their voices that call,
Among the black and the bellowing bones.

But yet when the cannibal
Sun is high
The sightless mud
Weeps tears, a sigh,
To rhinoceros-hided leaves: 'Ah why
So sightless, earless, voiceless, I?'

The mud has at least its skulls to roll;
But here as I walk, no voices call,
Only the stones and the bones that fall;
But yet if only one soul would whine,
Ratlike from the lowest mud, I should know
That somewhere in God's vast love it would shine;
But even the rat-whine has guttered low.

I saw the Blind like a winding-sheet
Tossed up and down through the blind man's street
Where the dead plague-spot
Of the spirit's rot
On the swollen thick houses
Cries to the quick,
Cries to the dark soul that lies there and dies
In hunger and murk, and answers not.

Gomorrah's fires have washed my blood—
But the fires of God shall wash the mud
Till the skin drums rolling
The slum cries sprawling
And crawling
Are calling
'Burn thou me!'
Though Death has taken
And piglike shaken
Rooted and tossed
The rags of me.
Yet the time will come
To the heart's dark slum
When the rich man's gold and the rich man's wheat
Will grow in the street, that the starved may eat—
And the sea of the rich will give up its dead—
And the last blood and fire from my side will be shed.
For the fires of God go marching on.

Song

TO JOHN AND ALEXANDRINE RUSSELL

Now that Fate is dead and gone
And that Madness reigns alone,
Still the Furies shake the fires
Of their torches in the street
Of my blood . . . And still they stand
In the city's street that tires
Of the tread of Man.

Three old rag-pickers are they—
Clothed with grandeur by the light
As a queen, but blind as Doom
Fumbling for the rag of Man
In an empty room.

Now they take the place of Fate
In whom the flames of Madness ran
Since her lidless eyes were cursed
With the world-expunging sight
Of the heart of Man.

How simple was the time of Cain
Before the latter Man-made Rain
Washed away all loss and gain
And the talk of right and wrong—
Murdered now and gone!

And the Ghost of Man is red
From the sweep of the world's blood. . . .

In this late equality
Would you know the Ghost of Man
From the Ghost of the Flea?

But still the fires of the great Spring
In the desolate fields proclaim
Eternity . . . those wild fires shout
Of Christ the New Song.

Run those fires from field to field;
I walk alone and ghostlily
Burning with Eternity's
Fires, and quench the Furies' song
In flame that never tires.

Eurydice

TO JOHN LEHMANN

Fires on the hearth! Fires in the heavens! Fires in the hearts of
      Men!
I who was welded into bright gold in the earth by Death
Salute you! All the weight of Death in all the world
Yet does not equal Love—the great compassion
For the fallen dust and all fallen creatures, quickening
As is the Sun in the void firmament.
It shines like fire. O bright gold of the heat of the Sun
Of Love across dark fields—burning away rough husks of Death
Till all is fire, and bringing all to harvest!

See then! I stand in the centre of my earth
That was my Death, under the zenith of my Sun
Bringing a word from Darkness
That Death too has compassion for all fallen Nature.
For as the Sun buries his hot days and rays
To ripen in earth, so the great rays of the heart
Are ripened to wisdom by Death, and great is our forgiveness.

When through the darkness Orpheus came with his Sunlike singing
Like the movements in the heavens that in our blindness
Could we but emulate, would set right our lives—
I came to the mouth of the Tomb, I did not know our meeting
      would be this:
—Only like the return at evening
Of the weary worker in the holy fields—
The cry of welcome, the remembered kiss!

In the lateness of the season, I with the golden feet
That had walked in the fields of Death, now walk again
The dark fields where the sowers scatter grain
Like tears, or the constellations that weep for the lateness of the
         season—
Where the women walk like mourners, like the Afternoon ripened,
        with their bent heads;
Their golden eyelids like the drifts of the narcissus
In spring, are wet with their tears. They mourn for a young wife
        who had walked these fields
—So young, not yet had Proserpina tied up her golden hair
In a knot like the branchèd corn. . . . So good was she—
With a voice like the sweet swallow. She lies in the silent Tomb

And they walk in the fields alone. Then one of the Dead who lay
Beneath the earth, like the water-dark, the water-thin
Effigy of Osiris, with a face green as a moon,
—He who was lying in darkness with the wheat
Like a flame springing from his heart, or a gold sound,
Said to me, 'We have been blind and stripped God naked of things
To see the light which shines in the dark, and we have learned
That the gold flame of the wheat may spring from a barren heart.'

When I came down from the Metropolis of the Corn,
Then said the ferine dust that reared about me,
'I have the famine of the lion, all things devour,
Or make them mine. . . . Venus was powerful as me—
Now is she but a handful of dry amber dust;
And my tooth cracked the husk, the dry amber wall
That held the fire of the wheat. That fire is gone—
And remember this, that Love, or I, have ground
Your heart between the stones of the years, like wheat.'

But as I left the mouth of the Tomb, far-off, like the noise of the
      dark wild bees,
I heard the sounds arise from the dwellings of Men, and I thought
      of their building,
Their wars, their honey-making, and of the gold roofs built against
      Darkness.

And I had learned beneath the earth that all gold nature
Changes to wheat or gold in the sweet darkness.
Why do they weep for those in the silent Tomb,
Dropping their tears like grain? Her heart, that honey-comb,
Thick Darkness like a bear devours. . . . See, all the gold is
      gone!
The cell of the honey-comb is six-sided. . . . But there, in the
      five cells of the senses,
Is stored all their gold. . . . Where is it now? Only the wind of
      the Tomb can know.
But I feared not that stilled and chilling breath
Among the dust. . . . Love is not changed by Death,
And nothing is lost and all in the end is harvest.

As the earth is heavy with the lion-strong Sun
When he has fallen, with his hot days and rays,
We are heavy with Death, as a woman is heavy with child,
As the corn-husk holds its ripeness, the gold comb
Its weight of summer. . . . But as if a lump of gold had changed
      to corn,
So did my life rise from my Death. I cast the grandeur of Death
      away
And homeward came to the small things of Love, the building of
      the hearth, the kneading of daily bread,
The cries of birth, and all the weight of light
Shaping our bodies and our souls. Came home to youth,
And the noise of summer growing in the veins,

And to old age, a serene afternoon,
An element beyond time, or a new climate.

I with the other young who were born from darkness,
Returning to darkness, stood at the mouth of the Tomb
With one who had come glittering like the wind
To meet me—Orpheus with the golden mouth,
You—like Adonis born from the young myrrh-tree, you, the vine-
     branch
Broken by the wind of love. . . . I turned to greet you—
And when I touched your mouth, it was the Sun.

A Sleepy Tune

TO VIOLET GORDON WOODHOUSE

'I was a Gold Man. . . . Now I lie under the earth
And only the young wheat-ear
Grows from my hollow breast like a gold sound . . .
Amid the asp-aspersions of the dust,
The old assertions
Of that sleep-causing Asp with swelling head.
And only the bull-voiced thunders of the gold ripe wheat
Answer the Augur in this long and sleepy August.'

The Gold Man who was King raised up his sleepy head. . . .
'Is this the time of our advance upon the Sun?
Will he kiss the loveless—
And stretch himself on our earth in love once more?
Lions do not bury gold and seek again
Their treasure . . . but the Sun sees our gold nature
Sunken in earth, and comes again to the Ore,
The growing plant and the root with the nature of gold
(Whose generation is in earth)—the Ore, precursor
Of the Plant Kingdom, that with growth becomes alive.

In the time when the Sun of the heart is in the sign of the Lion
I lie far from the forgotten thunders. . . .'
But near the Tomb, the Thriae, priestesses of the gold comb,
Buzz and hum of the forgotten wonders,
And of the wind from the Tomb that is no more
Than the wind of the honey-hive that drifts to them over their
        gold floor.

Their heads are white as if from barley-flour,
—And thin are their gold bodies.

This is the hour
When they sing of the noon of the world. 'There was a King
Who reigned in Babylon—
Grown sleepy now . . . His hair was like the honey-red foxes
Burned by fires like the Sun in the wheat-festival:—
He lies embalmed by bees . . . the sweetness lapping over
Him, with only Darkness for a lover. . . .
And now is his town no more than our gold comb.

And carrying a young lion,
A solar hero, King of Lydia,
Walked on his city walls. . . .
You would not know that King or lion now from the dust ground
          from the wheat-ears.

Great Alexander lies in a mask of gold
White honey mummified . . . as if it were gold armour.
And now only the cold
Wind from the honey-hive can know
If still from strength comes sweetness—if from the lion-heart
The winged swarms rise.'

This was the song of the Bee-Priestesses.
But the Gold Man lying in the dark like the wingless pupa
That lies in their cells, said 'I hear the solar jubilation
Come to the heart and saps of Being . . . the roar of ripeness.
For the Sun is the Ardent Belief
That sees life in the aridities of the dust,
In the seed and the base excrement and the world's fevers . . .
He loves alike the common dust of the streets
And the lovers' lips like the gold fires burning Troy.

The Sun kisses the loveless,
The mouth of the condemned by Man, the dog-mouth and the
        lion-fang
Deep in the heart. . . . He comes to the criminal whose nature
Was crippled before his birth by a new gravitation
That changed the solar system of the heart
To a universe reigned over by deformation . . .
None is condemned. . . . Then why should we lie loveless?
He will clothe us again in gold and a little love.'

The Bee-Keeper

TO DENYS AND ELIZABETH KILHAM ROBERTS

IN THE plain of the world's dust like a great Sea
The golden thunders of the Lion and the Honey-Bee
In the Spirit, held with the Sun a colloquy

Where an old woman stood—thick Earthiness—
Half Sun, half Clod,
A plant alive from the root, still blind with earth
And all the weight of Death and Birth.

She, in her primitive dress
Of clay, bent to her hives
And heard her sisters of the barren lives

Begin to stir. . . . The Priestesses of the gold comb
Shaped by Darkness, and the Prophetesses
Who from a wingless pupa, spark of gold

In the Dark, rose with gold bodies bright as the Lion,
And the trace of the Hand of God on ephemeral wings,
To sing the great Hymn of Being to the Lost:

'This Earth is the honey of all Beings, and all Beings
Are the honey of this Earth. . . . O bright immortal Lover
That is incarnate in the body's earth—
O bright immortal Lover who is All!'

'This Water is the honey of all Beings, and all Beings
Are the honey of this Water. . . . O the bright immortal Lover

That is in water and that is the seed
Of Life. . . . O bright immortal Lover who is All!'

'This Fire is the honey of all Beings and all Beings
Are the honey of this Fire. . . . O bright immortal Lover
That is in fire and shines in mortal speech—
O bright immortal Lover who is All!'

'This Air is the honey of all Beings and all Beings
Are the honey of this Air. . . . O bright immortal Lover
That is in air and is our Being's breath—
O bright immortal Lover who is All!'

'This Sun is the honey of all Beings and all Beings
Are the honey of this Sun. . . . O bright immortal Lover
That is in the Sun and is our Being's sight—
O bright immortal Lover who is All!'

'This Thunder is the honey of all Beings and all Beings
Are the honey of this Thunder. . . . O the bright immortal Lover
That is in thunder and all voices—the beasts' roar
—Thunders of rising saps, the voice of Man!
O bright immortal Lover who is All!'

This was the song that came from the small span
Of thin gold bodies shaped by the holy Dark.

And the old woman in her mortal dress of clay
(That plant alive from the root, still thick with earth)
Felt all the saps of Day;

And in the plain of dust like a great Sea
The Lion in the Spirit cried 'Destroy—destroy
The old and wrinkled Darkness!' But the Sun—

That great gold simpleton, laughed like a boy,
And kissed the old woman's cheek and blessed her clay.

The great Sun laughed, and dancing over Chaos
Shouts to the dust 'O mortal Lover! Think what wonders
May be born of our love—what golden heroes!'

The Bee in the Spirit said 'The gold combs lay
In the cold rock and the slain Lion, amid spent golden thunders!'

ᴺotes

THE SHADOW OF CAIN

Verse 5. Lines 2 and 3

Arthur Rimbaud: "Metropolitan"

Verse 19. Lines 3 and 4

"And bull-voices roar thereto from somewhere out of the Unseen, fearful mimes, and from a drum an image, as it were, of thunder underground is borne on the air heavy with dread."

A fragment of the lost Edoniaus of Aeschylus, preserved by Strabo (quoted by Dr. Jane Ellen Harrison in *Ancient Art and Ritual*). The fragment refers to the worshippers of Dionysus. I have used the image in the sense of the noise of rising saps and the Spring.

Verse 20. Line 3

"Irenaeus expressed it so elegantly as it is almost pity if it be not true: 'Inseminatus est ubique in Scripturis, Filius Dei,' says he: 'The Son of God is sowed in every furrow.' "—John Donne: *Sermon XI*.

Verse 21. Line 6

After the Atomic Bomb fell on Hiroshima, according to eye-witnesses, dust rose to the sun in the shape of a totem-pole—the symbol of life.

Verse 30. Lines 2, 3, 4, and 5

Descriptions by Lombroso and Havelock Ellis of prenatally disposed criminals. Verses 27, 31, 34, 35, and 36 contain references to certain Alchemical Writings.

Verse 39. Lines 2 and 3

John Donne: *Sermon CXXXVI*.

THE CANTICLE OF THE ROSE

Verses 2 and 3 contain references to Lorenz Oken's *Elements of Physiophilosophy*.

Verse 12. Lines 4 and 5

Milton: *Paradise Lost:* Book III.
Line 9. *The Anturs of Artur.*
Line 10. Wycliff: *Selected Writings.*

THE TWO LOVES

Verse 4. Lines 28, 29, 30

'. . . Tell the blind
The hue of the flower, or the philosopher
What distance is, in the essence of its being.'
—A paraphrase of a passage by William James.

Verse 5. Line 5

'Umbilical cords that bind us to strange suns'
—A paraphrase of a sentence by a French author—I do not know his name.

Verse 5. Lines 7 and 8

'Bless Jesus Christ with the Rose and his people, which is a nation of living
sweetness.'—CHRISTOPHER SMART: "Rejoice with the Lamb."

Verse 5. Lines 15, 16, 17, 18

These came into my head after reading a passage in Lorenz Oken's *Elements of
Physiophilosophy*; the lines are in part a transcript.

A HYMN TO VENUS

Verse 2. Line "seeds of petrifaction, Gorgon of itself."—Sir Thomas Browne:
Of Vulgar Errors.

METAMORPHOSIS

Verse 45. Lines 1 and 2.

Dryden: "Annus Mirabilis."

Verse 55. Line 2

'The Word was from the beginning, and therefore was and is the divine beginning of all things, but now that He has taken the name, which of old was sancti-
fied, the Christ, He is called by me a New Song.'—St. Clement: "Address to the
Greeks."

Verse 56. Lines 3 and 4

'The Lord, having taken upon Him all the infirmities of our body, is then
covered with the scarlet-coloured blood of all the martyrs.'—St. Hilary quoted by
St. Thomas Aquinas: *Catena Aurea.*

STREET ACROBAT
Verse 12. Line 1
. . . lie immortal in the arms of Fire.—Sir Thomas Browne.
Verse 12. Lines 3 and 4
. . . a tight rope stretched from beast to God . . .—is an adaptation of a line from Nietzsche. But there it was 'Superman' not 'God.'

THE SONG OF THE COLD
Verse 1. Line 2
'There was the morning when, with Her, you struggled amongst those banks of snow, those green-lipped crevasses, that ice, those black flags and blue rays, and purple perfumes of the polar sun. . . .'—Arthur Rimbaud: "Metropolitan" (translated by Helen Rootham).
Verse 1. Lines 6 and 7
'This evening, Devotion to Circeto of the tall mirrors, fat as a fish and glowing like the ten months of the red night (her heart is of amber and musk)—for me a prayer, mute as those regions of night. . . .'—Arthur Rimbaud: "Devotion."
Verse 5. Line 1, et seq.
The Miser Foscue, a Farmer General of France, existing in Languedoc about 1760. These lines tell his actual story.

THE COAT OF FIRE
Lines 21, 22, 23, contain references to the Tibetan *Book of the Dead.* Lines 53 to 66 refer to the Buddha's Fire Sermon.

GOLD COAST CUSTOMS
'The Negroes indulge that perfect contempt for humanity which in its bearing on Justice and Morality is the fundamental characteristic of the race. They have, moreover, no knowledge of the immortality of the soul, although spectres are supposed to appear. The undervaluing of humanity among them reaches an incredible degree of intensity. Tyranny is regarded as no wrong, and cannibalism is looked upon as quite customary and proper. Among us instinct deters from it, if we can speak of instinct at all as appertaining to man. But with the Negro this is not the case, and the devouring of human flesh is altogether consonant with the general principles of the African race; to the sensual Negro, human flesh is but an object of sense—mere flesh. At the death of a king hundreds are killed and

eaten; prisoners are butchered and their flesh sold in the market place; the victor is accustomed to eat the flesh of his fallen foe.'—Hegel: *Philosophy of History*.

It is needless to add that this refers only to a past age, and that, in quoting this passage, I intend no reflection whatever upon the African races of our time. This passage no more casts a reflection upon them than a passage referring to the cruelties of the Tudor age casts a reflection upon the English of our present age. E.S.

Verse 1. *Line* 5

'Munza rattles his bones in the dust.' King Munza reigned, in 1874, over the Monbuttoo, a race of cannibals in Central Africa. These notes are taken from Dr. Georg Schweinfurth's *The Heart of Africa* (translated by Ellen Frewer, published by Messrs. Sampson Low). Of the Monbuttoo and their neighbours the Niam-Niam, we read: "Human fat is universally sold. . . . Should any lone and solitary individual die, uncared for . . . he would be sure to be devoured in the very district in which he lived. During our residence at the Court of Munza the general rumour was quite current that nearly every day some little child was sacrificed to supply his meal. There are cases in which bearers who died from fatigue had been dug out of the graves in which they had been buried . . . in order that they might be devoured. The cannibalism of the Monbuttoo is the most pronounced of all the known nations of Africa. Surrounded as they are by a number of people who, being inferior to them in culture, are consequently held in great contempt, they have just the opportunity which they want for carrying on expeditions of war and plunder, which result in the acquisition of a booty which is especially coveted by them, consisting of human flesh. But with it all, the Monbuttoos are a noble race of men, men who display a certain national pride . . . men to whom one may put a reasonable question and receive a reasonable answer. The Nubians can never say enough in praise of their faithfulness in friendly intercourse and of the order and stability of their national life. According to the Nubians, too, the Monbuttoos were their superiors in the arts of war."

Verse 23. *Line* 2, *et seq.*

'And her soul, the cannibal Amazon's mart.'

'Tradition alleges that in former times a state composed of women made itself famous by its conquests: it was a state at whose head was a woman. She is said to have pounded her son in a mortar, and to have had the blood of pounded children constantly at hand. She is said to have driven away or put to death all the males, and commanded the death of all male children. These furies destroyed everything in the neighbourhood, and were driven to constant plunderings because they did not cultivate the land. . . . This infamous state, the report goes on to say, subsequently disappeared.'—Hegel: *Philosophy of History*, chapter on Africa.

EURYDICE
Verse 4. Lines 8, 9, and 10

. . . 'A most sweet wife, a young wife, Nondum sustulerat flavum Proserpina crinem (not yet has Proserpina tied up her golden hair)—such a wife as no man ever had, so good a wife, but she is now dead and gone, Lethaeoque jacet condita sarcophago (she lies buried in the silent tomb).'—Robert Burton: *The Anatomy of Melancholy.*

Verse 5. Lines 6 and 7

'The light which God is shines in darkness, God is the true light: to see it one has to be blind and strip God naked of things.'—Meister Eckhart: *Sermons and Collations, XIX.*

Verse 9. Lines 3 and 4

'And her deadness
Was filling her with fullness
Full as a fruit with sweetness and darkness
Was she with her great death.'

R. M. Rilke (translated by J. B. Leishmann). . . .

A SLEEPY TUNE
Verse 2. Line 5

"When shall you see a lion hide gold in the ground?"—Robert Burton: *The Anatomy of Melancholy.*

Verse 5

An ancient Persian manuscript speaks of drowning and embalming a red-haired man in honey.

Verse 6

The tale of Alexander the Great King embalmed in white honey occurs more than once in Sir Ernest Wallis Bridges' *Life and Exploits of Alexander the Great.*

THE BEE-KEEPER

The verses 9 to 11 are founded on the great Second Adhyaha of the Brihadāranyaka Upanishad:

'This earth is the honey (madhu, the effect) of all beings, and all beings are the honey or madhu, the effect of this earth. Likewise the bright immortal person incorporated in the body (both are madhu). He indeed is the same as that Self, that Immortal, that Brahman, that All.', etc.

I have founded the lines on this great Hymn with all reverence.

113